# = WE'LL RING IN GOD'S NAME. =

A Journey with Jeanne Jugan

A Saint for Our Time!

by
Joan Thiry
illustrated by
Stephen Titra

# Dedication

To The Little Sisters of the Poor, the "little Jeanne Jugans" worldwide,
but especially to those serving us at St. Mary Home and Jugan Terrace
in Chicago, with great love,
I dedicate this Journey with
St. Jeanne Jugan.
Joan Thiry

# Acknowledgements

I gratefully acknowledge and bless all who supported me in this en-
deavor with their insights, their encouragement and their financial aid,
especially The Little Sisters of the Poor, Stephen Titra,
Steve and Jeanne Karabin, Thomas Drabant, Michael Janet,
Barbara Fleeman Hazlett, Barbara, Christopher and Ellie Raam,
Mary Rose Lehr, Charles Fleeman, Robert and Marietta Walsh,
Alois Becker, Arthur Becker, Margaret Mary and John Conley,
Michael and D'Neil Duffy, Marlene and Leo Leonardi,
James Gerard Smith and all Anonymous Donors

ISBN Number 0-935046-06-2

Published in the USA by Chateau Thierry Press, 2300 N. Racine Ave., Ste. 409, Chicago, IL 60614.
Printed by Weber Press. Inc., Chicago, IL

"I can't beg! I don't want to!" said Claire to Jeanne. But Jeanne answered her.
"I don't want to either, but I'll be a 'beggar maid' for the elderly poor. We'll ring in God's Name!"
And Jeanne pulled the door bell cord.

Did doors open for Jeanne Jugan and her "beggar maids"?
Let's look inside and see.

Jeanne's father was a sailor. The family lived in a village called La Petites Croix, near Cancale, Brittany, France. Jeanne was born in 1792 at a time when France had a big revolution. Almost everyone was poor. The family waited many years for a ship to bring their father home. He never came.

While Jeanne's family watched for their sailor father to come home, they all worked hard to pay the rent and buy food they couldn't grow, like flour and salt.

Everyone helped in Jeanne's home. Mother washed clothes and cleaned homes of rich people. In winter, she spun wool or flax and made clothes for the children. Jeanne and her sister Therese knitted stockings to sell. Their brother was too young to be a cabin boy so he cared for the family animals. All helped prepare the evening meal. Therese-Charlotte helped by playing with the cat.

Each evening before the family ate their meal, they prayed the rosary to honor the Blessed Mother. After their meal, mother often taught them catechism, stories about Jesus and the sacraments. Remember that churches were closed. Mother also taught them their school lessons because they couldn't always get to school. They learned songs, too. Jeanne loved to sing.

On Easter Sunday, 1802, when Jeanne was only 10 years old, Napoleon, Emperor of France and Pope Pius VII agreed to open the churches in France. Jeanne and many children made their first Holy Communion. Jeanne was very happy. The next year, 1803, Bishop de Maille came to a nearby church, Saint Servan and confirmed 1500 baptized Catholics including Jeanne and her family.

When Jeanne was 18 years old, she went to work as a kitchen maid at a large estate, called The Screeching Owl. She was a good worker and cared about the family for whom she cooked. She would feed the poor whenever they came to the kitchen door.

Often she joined Madame de La Choue on trips to the village to help the elderly and poor.

A French-Canadian sailor who lived in Cancale when he was in port often saw the two women visit the homes of the sick and poor. He could see how gentle and respectful Jeanne was to those she helped.

One day, he introduced himself and asked her to marry him. It was a custom in Cancale for the man to propose marriage but the couple would wait a few years before marrying. Jeanne told him she was surprised by his proposal because she was no one special. Still, she asked him to wait.

Jeanne's sailor came from Newfoundland, Canada. Perhaps he sometimes was on the same ship as Jeanne's father.

With the churches open again, priests began "parish missions" – special days when people went to church to pray, sing and learn about Jesus. In 1816, when Jeanne was 24, a "mission" came to Cancale. She prayed and sang and loved it. And she did some thinking too.

Just then, Jeanne's sailor came back to ask her again to marry him. He had waited six years. She told the sailor, gently, that she could not marry him because, she said, "God wants me for himself. He's keeping me for a work as yet unknown, for a work which is not yet founded."

In the spring of 1816, Jeanne's older sister, Marie Joseph married William Partier. About a year later, her little sister, Therese Charlotte, married Joseph Emery. Jeanne gave each of them her good clothes as a wedding present. She then moved to Saint Servan, a nearby town, to work in St. Rosais, the hospital there. She was 25 years old and ready to search for her future work.

It was a very poor time in France. In Saint Servan, at that time, there were over four thousand (4,000) poor begging, homeless people. The big hospital tried to help everyone – the sick, orphan children, widows, and homeless elderly – all.  Jeanne was a nurse. Later she learned to mix medicines and became a pharmacist.  Jeanne worked very hard.

Jeanne's work with the sick and poor brought her closer to Jesus and His Mother, Mary. Jeanne asked a priest how she could grow more like Jesus and Mary. The priest explained that he was a member of the "Society of the Heart of Mary" and they had a special part for lay people – not priests or sisters, but a "third order". Jeanne joined others in this group. They prayed together and learned about God's love from the priests of St. John Eudes. Jeanne was happy with these good friends.

Jeanne worked so hard at the hospital that she became sick from exhaustion. Miss Lecoq saw how worn out Jeanne was. She took Jeanne to her home and put her to bed. Miss Lecoq nursed Jeanne back to health. While Jeanne was getting stronger, Miss Lecoq invited Jeanne to stay and live with her.

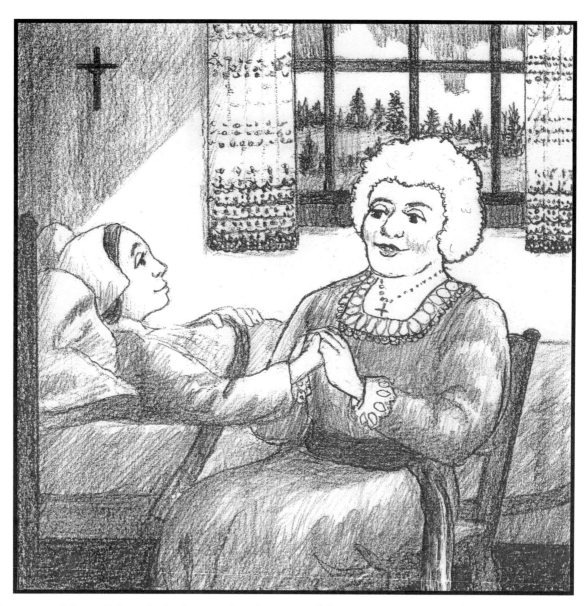

They could still both help in the hospital but Jeanne would have a clean bed and good food at Miss Lecoq's home

Jeanne and Miss Lecoq visited the poor and elderly. They brought food and even medicine, if they could. In the evenings they prayed together or read good books. Jeanne and Miss Lecoq helped at the hospital for twelve years until Miss Lecoq died in 1835.

Jeanne also taught the children who lived at the hospital about God. They called this 'catechism lessons.' Jeanne made up songs to teach the children about Jesus. She also taught them songs they would sing in church. The children loved to sing about Jesus with Jeanne.

Jeanne was about 45 years old now and she had to earn a living. She worked as a nurse, a cleaning lady, a washerwoman – whatever she could find. Jeanne had an older friend, Francoise Aubert, who was 72. Francoise spun wool to earn a living. Together they rented a two-room flat near the church. They worked all day and in the evening, they shared a meal, their prayers and conversation.

One day, a good man brought Virginie Tredaniel, an orphan of 17, to Jeanne. He asked if Virginie could live with Jeanne. Jeanne and Francoise welcomed Virginie, who was a seamstress. So in 1838, these three ladies began their shared life of work, prayer and helping the poor.

During the cold winter of 1839, Jeanne saw so many poor, shivering old people on her walk to work that she made a very big decision. She decided that she would quit her job with the good Leroy family, who loved and cared about her. From then on, she would work every day to help the poor.

"How will you do this, Jeanne? You have no money." Asked Mr. Leroy. "I will beg." replied Jeanne, "and I will begin with you." The kind Leroys gave Jeanne 300 francs, her first gift for the elderly poor.

Soon afterward, on a cold December day in 1839, Jeanne was coming home from work when she saw an old lady shivering in the doorway of a building. Jeanne stopped to talk to her. The old lady was Anne Chauvin. She was almost blind and was homeless. Jeanne carried Anne to her little bedroom. Jeanne put Anne in her own bed. That night, Jeanne fed Anne and made sure she was warm and comfortable. Only then did Jeanne make a straw bed for herself up in the cold attic.

That was the beginning of the Christian work of Jeanne and her two companions, Francoise and Virginie. For the rest of their lives, they would care for the elderly poor.

Before very long, Jeanne, Francoise and Virginie took in another homeless woman, Isabelle. Soon after that, they took in Madeleine whom they nursed back to health. Madeleine joined their little group.

A friend of Virginie, named Marie Jamet, grew vegetables for them. She often joined them for prayer and their discussions. Finally, she joined them in their "big downstairs". These young ladies asked Jeanne to write a little "rule" or "way of life" for them, like the "Third Order Way" that Jeanne followed. Jeanne did. Around this time, a priest Marie Jamet knew, Father LePailleur, saw what good work they were doing and became their director.

Now there were four of them in their association – Jeanne, Virginie, Marie and Madeleine. Francoise said she was too old but she lived with them, as well as Anne and Isabelle.

Their two rooms were much too small.  So, in the summer of 1841, Jeanne and her associates found a "big downstairs" as they called it.  It was a dark, damp, empty basement, but it had room for twelve beds, plus a storeroom for food and a room for them, the associates, to work, pray, laugh and sleep.  Jeanne paid 100 francs for a year's rent.  Everyone helped carry their furniture into the "big downstairs" and set up their new home.

That same day, four poor, old ladies begged to join them and were welcomed.  Soon all twelve beds were filled.  The work Jeanne knew God had asked of her had really begun.  Their parish priest blest their home and its residents.  Jeanne prayed, "Blest be God!"

How would they feed and clothe all these elderly poor?  Anne, Isabelle and Madeleine were better now.  They spent their time spinning wool and hemp.  Virginie contributed the money she made by dressmaking.  Marie Jamet contributed vegetables; but they would need more food and money.

One day, Jeanne met a young man out begging for food.  He was called a "Brother of St. John of God", a Catholic group that cared for the sick and handicapped.  "We go begging.  People are often generous." said the Brother.  "I couldn't beg.  I'm too ashamed." replied Jeanne.  "It's not for you." said the Brother.  "It's for the poor.  Here is my begging basket.  I give it to you with my blessing."

So Jeanne and her companions became "beggar maids for God", as Jeanne called them.  Jeanne would take a deep breath, look at the doorbell, smile and say, "We'll ring in God's name!"

Daily their needs grew.  Many needy elderly joined their family. Then in September, these "Servants of the Poor" were able, with the help of a rich man, to buy a bigger house.  Now they could welcome men, also.

Virginie and Madeleine took care of the residents and the home.  Jeanne and Marie did most of the begging.  They accepted everything – leftovers, vegetables, clothing, precious items, like salt.

One day, Jeanne saw the residents eating dry bread.  "We have no butter for them.", said Virginie.  Jeanne collected all the butter dishes and put them in front of St. Joseph's statue.  She said, "We live in the land of butter.  St. Joseph will find some."  Not long after, the doorbell rang and a dairyman brought a crock of butter.  St. Joseph always seemed to provide.

St. Joseph had the butter brought to the door, but Jeanne had to work for it when she went out to find some tasty bacon for her family. Jeanne and Marie wanted to buy a pig that would grow big and give them a winter's supply of bacon and pork roasts.

There were pigs for sale, but all they could afford was a sickly piglet. They had to carry it home in their arms it was so weak and sickly. The piglet was given such good care that eventually he weighed 200 pounds and produced a lot of bacon and pork roast. Another time a ship owner, Monsieur de Gouyon, sent the home 1220 pounds of salt bacon that he could not ship overseas. The happy residents had bacon with their eggs for a long time. St. Joseph, once again, provided!

Jeanne cared about giving her dear elderly folks happy entertainment, as well as delicious food. She did this once in a while for a special day, a feast day or holiday.  So, in Angers, Jeanne went one day to the soldier garrison and timidly asked the colonel in command if he would send two or three members of his band to entertain her old folk on the feast day that was coming.

"Sister, to please you and make your beloved old folk happy, I'll send you the whole band!" replied the smiling colonel.

The Angers brass band brought smiles and laughter to all old folk and sisters that feast day!  It made the old people feel important!  After all, the famous Army band had played especially for them.

Not everyone was kind and generous to Jeanne and her "Servants of the Poor." One angry man told Jeanne to get off his land or he would send his dogs after her. Another man slapped Jeanne. She said, "That was for me. Now, please, give me something for my poor."

Jeanne even went to the horseraces or to the beaches to beg. One rich lady told Jeanne that she was spoiling her good time. "Don't be so stingy.", said her husband, as he gave Jeanne some francs for her poor. "I made this money betting on the boat races."

One day when Jeanne was begging along the seashore, she met her sea captain friend, Monsieur de Guyon, the ship owner who had given them over a thousand pounds of bacon. He looked very upset. His sailors were unloading a shipment of gold. A bag of gold had fallen into the water. The sailors could not find it. Jeanne told him they would find it and she went along the shore. When she returned later, the ship owner was smiling and holding the dripping bag of gold.

"I told you, dear Monsieur de Guyon, that God would make you recover your money." said Jeanne. Smiling, the kind ship owner handed Jeanne the bag of gold worth 10,000 francs. "Here," he said, "take the bag. This is for your little, old folk."

10,000 francs was a wonderful gift! It could buy a new home for Jeanne's poor.

Everyone knew Jeanne Jugan and how she helped the poor elderly. Once, when Jeanne went to beg from the hundreds of shipbuilders working in the shipyards, the foreman spoke to Jeanne. "Our men want to help you feed and care for the poor, old people you take into your homes. So, each of us will give you a penny a week. I collect these as the shipbuild- ers come into the yards. Here is our bag of coins for the week. Please come again next week and every week after that. We care about these old people. Some of our grandmothers or grandfathers might be among them."

Jeanne said her usual prayer as she accepted the bag of coins. She said, "Thank you, God." and "Praise God."

We don't know how much a "penny" or "centime" was at that time, around 1845 in France, but every penny helped, just as it still does today in homes of the "Little Sisters of the Poor."

Each year the French Academy gave an award, called the Montyon Award to someone who was poor and still helped others who were poor. In Saint Servan, the parish priest, the mayor and other important people wrote and signed their tribute to Jeanne Jugan. Jeanne did not want her name mentioned, but finally said, "Yes." The award would bring much needed money as well as honor. In 1845, Jeanne won this award and received 6,000 francs for her homes. Newspapers wrote about Jeanne and the work of her Servants of the Poor. Because of this good publicity, more towns and cities asked for homes. More people were willing to help Jeanne's poor.

Jeanne's companions, Virginie, Marie and Madeleine, wanted to join Jeanne in a way of life more like religious sisters lead. Around 1842 these women took a vow – a promise – of obedience. They had already promised not to marry. Another promise was hospitality, to welcome and serve the elderly poor. These women elected Jeanne as their leader for a year. In 1843, Jeanne was elected leader again. She, after all, had begun this work.

Then a strange thing happened. Father Le Pailleur, their director, said he did not want Jeanne in charge. Instead, he put Marie Jamet, only 23 years old, in charge. He sent Jeanne out begging. The sisters, including

Jeanne, quietly accepted their priest's decision. Later on, he even pretended that he had started the Little Sisters of the Poor. Only after Jeanne's death, some 30 years later, did the truth of the community's beginnings become known.

News of Jeanne Jugan's good work spread.  A famous Christian journalist, Louis Veuillot, wrote glowing stories about Jeanne and her "little Jeanne Jugans", as many people lovingly called her companions.  Soon requests for homes came in from other cities in France.

One day, an English tourist visited Jeanne.  He asked to see her home for the Poor.  We think he was the famous writer, Charles Dickens.  He was so impressed by Jeanne's happy, old people that when he got back to England, he wrote all about Jeanne and her good work.  "We need this in England," he said.  "Please come to our country."  So, in 1851, the Little Sisters made their first home outside of France – in England.

The community of Little Sisters of the Poor kept growing. They needed a bigger home. St. Joseph helped the Sisters get the 212,000 francs they needed to buy a big estate, called La Tour, in St. Pern, France. This was in January 1856. Three Little Sisters arrived in April, 1856. They named their new home "St. Joseph". It took twenty years just to make the repairs needed on all the buildings.

This is where Jeanne Jugan, now known as Sister Marie of the Cross, came in April, 1856. Jeanne would live there among the postulants and novices, young ladies learning to be Sisters, until her death in 1879.

Today La Tour St. Joseph is still the motherhouse, the heart of the community of the Little Sisters of the Poor. You can see La Tour for yourself by going on www.littlesistersofthepoor.org.

On most of her days at La Tour, Jeanne joined the novices in the sewing room where she knitted stockings for the old people. Jeanne would tell the young Sisters the same thing over and over. She would say, **"WE MUST ALWAYS SAY 'BLESSED BE GOD.'"** or **"THANK YOU MY GOD**

Jeanne understood that to love God is to praise and give thanks! Jeanne had another way of thanking God when people gave her food or money. She would say to the person, "Let us say a Hail Mary together." Jeanne loved to pray her rosary which she always had with her. Once Jeanne said, "The Hail Mary will take us to heaven.

Sister Marie of the Cross had no special job at La Tour St. Joseph. She often took long walks with the young people studying to be Sisters. Jeanne loved to sing church songs. She loved folk songs, too. Maybe she sang "Frére Jacques" with the novices.

From Jeanne, Sister Marie of the Cross, these new Little Sisters learned a spirit of praising and thanking God always, both in prayer and in song. Jeanne shared her wisdom with these young Sisters. Directly from her, they learned to be happy "beggar maids for Christ."

These early Little Sisters of the Poor, and especially Jeanne, Sister Marie of the Cross, had a special priest friend who was a great blessing to them. His name was Father Ernest Lelievre. He was so inspired by Jeanne's work with the poor that after he was ordained a priest in 1855, he chose to devote his life to helping Jeanne and her Sisters serve the poor. He did this for 35 years until his death in 1889.

Father's family and he himself were very rich. He not only used his own money; he coaxed his relatives to use theirs to help the poor. Father was also a lawyer, so he was often a big help in getting governments to give permission when the Little Sisters wanted to start homes in a foreign country. He helped them establish homes in England, Belgium, Malta, Spain, Ireland, the United States, North Africa and Italy.

Each time he returned from a trip, Father would visit Sister Marie of the Cross. He would tell her how their many homes were doing. During his 35 years of helping, Father was part of establishing over 200 homes. Jeanne's work was blossoming.

Sister Marie of the Cross did very ordinary things during her days at La Tour. Yet, once in a while, something amazing would happen. Some might call it a "miracle".

Once, Sister Marie of the Cross was out walking with the novices when they heard the workmen calling, " Run, Sisters, run! A mad bull is loose." Then Jeanne said, "No! Lie down on the ground, Sisters." They quickly did. Jeanne faced the charging bull, held up her cane and called, "Stop!" The bull stopped and the workmen were able to take it back to its pen.

Another time Jeanne was praying in the chapel, when a mother carried in her 5-year old son who had never walked. Her other healthy children were with her. As she always did, the mother prayed that her little boy be cured. Leaving the chapel, she was still carrying him. Jeanne met her and took the child from the mother. She held him a moment and then put him down saying, "Little one, what a weight you are!"

Jeanne handed the child her cane. He took it and began to walk on his own. "Little John is walking!" cried the Mother. "He's walking with Jeanne Jugan's stick." Jeanne was a person who lived always aware of God and at times God's power acted through her.

Sister Marie of the Cross, Jeanne Jugan, lived at La Tour St. Joseph for 23 years. During her last years, Jeanne was almost blind, so she lived in the sisters' infirmary, the area of special care for those too frail to care for themselves. Jeanne spent much of her time praying. She also still shared her wisdom, her songs and her laughter with the younger sisters.

Jeanne longed to go to God, to be with Jesus and Mary in heaven, but she still had one last wish for her community. Her good friend, Father Lelievre, helped her with that. In November 1878, he went to Rome and personally gave the "Rules of the Little Sisters" to Pope Leo XIII. Father begged the Pope to approve both the Rules and the community. The Pope said, "Yes." and after the Rules were reviewed, Pope Leo XIII approved the Little Sisters' rules and community on March 1st, 1879.

Jeanne's wish was granted! How happy she and Father Lelievre must have been! She was especially happy because Father also told her that at that time there were over 2,400 Little Sisters serving the poor – only 40 years after Jeanne took in blind Anne.

Now Jeanne could say that her work on earth was done.  She was ready to go to Jesus and Mary.  On August 29, 1879, Jeanne Jugan died peacefully.  She was buried in a simple grave.

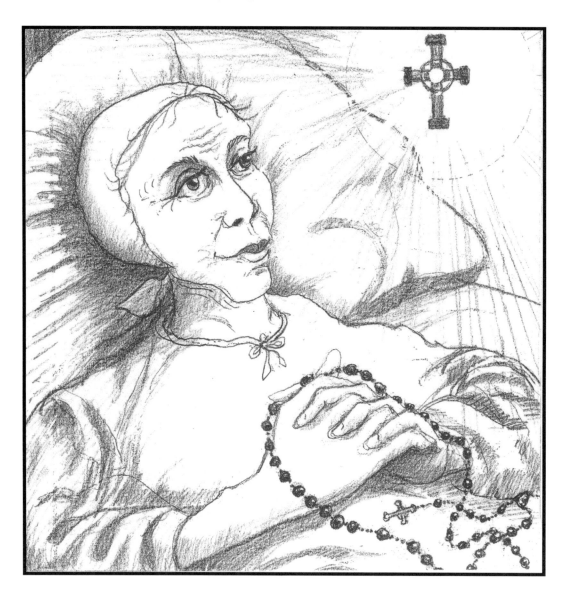

Was she to be forgotten?

No! Jeanne's good work for the elderly poor grew and grew. Many homes were opened in France. Remember, too, that as early as 1851, the Little Sisters opened their first home in England. In 1868 they came to New York. Then, in 1876, the Little Sisters came to Chicago. They have about 30 homes in the United States.

Father Lelievre could, happily, tell Jeanne about the new homes being started around the world because he was usually the one to make the long boat trips to foreign countries to get government approval, to find a building and get things ready for the Little Sisters who came.

As early as 1855, he told Jeanne that she had over 100 homes already in France and Spain, and that he would soon be going to Ireland, America and North Africa. Before his death in 1889, Father Lelievre had helped establish homes in Great Britain, Belgium, Malta, Spain, Ireland, the United States, North Africa and Italy. In 1882, eight Little Sisters went to Calcutta, India. Today, the Little Sisters have homes on five continents, including many in Asia, Africa, Australia and New Zealand.

Remember how the little boy who hadn't walked in five years, began to walk with Jeanne's cane? God showed power through Jeanne, even when she was still living. God continues to show power through Jeanne Jugan now that she is in heaven. We know that many prayers are answered when someone prays to Jeanne Jugan to intercede with Jesus on his behalf.

Two special answers to prayer have been considered "miracles" by the officials in the Vatican who decide these things. Around 1982, a man named Antoine Schlatter, who lived at the Little Sisters in Toulon, France, was told he would have to have his one hand amputated because of his Raynaud disease. Everyone prayed to Jeanne Jugan for him and he was cured.

A second "miracle" happened in Omaha, Nebraska in the United States in 1989. Friends of Dr. Gatz, M.D. prayed to Blessed Jeanne Jugan to cure him of his cancer of the esophagus. God heard their prayers and he was cured. Even today, Dr. Gatz is cancer-free.

Jeanne Jugan was declared "Blessed Jeanne Jugan" by Pope John Paul II on October 3, 1982. Her life was considered heroically holy.

Saint Jeanne Jugan

Sister Marie De la Croix

1792 - 1879

We must always say "Blessed Be God." "Thank You My God." "Glory be to God."

On October 11, 2009, the bells of St. Peter's Basilica in Rome were ringing to announce a great event. Along with others, His Holiness, POPE BENEDICT XVI, declared Blessed Jeanne Jugan, foundress of the Little Sisters of the Poor, SAINT JEANNE JUGAN.

Gathered in St. Peter's Square to join in the celebration were great throngs of joyous pilgrims. Among them were many Little Sisters of the Poor, daughters of Saint Jeanne Jugan. Joining the sisters were elderly people who live in homes belonging to the Little Sisters. All these joined thousands of other joyful pilgrims participating in this great event.

We too can join our voices to those of the pilgrims, praising and thanking God for this great blessing. We can pray with Saint Jeanne Jugan,

# "GOD IS GOOD! BLESSED BE GOD!"

Once there was a little girl who didn't want to go to sleep, so she came to the top of the stairs and called, "Mommy! Daddy! Come up to me! I'm all by myself."

"No, you're not." reassured the Mother from the bottom of the stairs. "God is with you and your doll."

The little girl exclaimed, "I don't want just God and my dolly! I WANT SOMEONE WITH SKIN ON!"

Old people are often lonely. Poor, old people can be even lonelier. They maybe can't afford to join clubs or travel on trips. Yes, many of them pray. Often they pray many rosaries a day. And they have their precious treasures and memories – photo albums, cards made by grandchildren who, perhaps, are too busy to visit now. Like the little girl, they 'WANT SOMEONE WITH SKIN ON!'

Today, all around the world, nearly 3,000 Little Sisters are those 'someones with skin on' who care for the elderly poor. They have expanded their care to include homes for 'independent living' for elderly poor people who can still care for themselves. They even invite the senior citizens in the neighborhood to join Home members for Sunday or feastday dinners and activities.

The Little Sisters have many helpers as they serve the elderly. People who care come to help serve Sunday dinner or to go with a sick person to the doctor or help them play games. There are never enough helpers.

Perhaps you, too, would like to help! To find some ways, visit the website of the Little Sisters of the Poor at www.littlesistersofthepoor.org.

And please, don't forget to visit the elderly in your family and in your neighborhood.

# A Saint

Saint Jeanne
Jugan

Sister Marie
De la Croix

1792 - 1879

We must
always say
"Blessed Be God."
"Thank You
My God."
"Glory be
to God."

# For Our Time

Jesus, You rejoiced and praised Your Father for having revealed to little ones the mysteries of the Kingdom of Heaven.  We thank You for the graces granted to Your humble servant, Jeanne Jugan, to whom we confide our petitions and needs.

Father of the Poor, You have never refused the prayer of the lowly.  We ask You, therefore, to hear the petitions that she presents to You on our behalf.

Jesus, through Mary, Your Mother and ours, we ask this of You, who live and reign with the Father and the Holy Spirit now and forever.  Amen

Saint Jeanne Jugan
Foundress of the Little Sisters of the Poor
(1792 – 1879)